Secrets of Shellfishing

Secrets of Shellfishing

by Edward R. Ricciuti

ISBN 0-88839-140-4

Copyright © 1982 Edward R. Ricciuti

Cataloging in Publication Data

Ricciuti, Edward R.
  Secrets of shellfishing
  (Northeast fishing series)

  1. Shellfish Gathering. I. Title
  II. Series
  SH400.4.R53   799.2'55384   C82-091151-8

All rights reserved. No part of this publication may be reproduced, stored in a retrieval system or transmitted, in any form or by any means, electronic, mechanical, photocopying, recording or otherwise, without the prior written permission of Hancock House Publishers.

Editor Nancy Flight
Typeset by Lisa Smedman in Garamond type on an AM
   Varityper Comp/Edit
Layout Linda Rourke
Production & Cover Design Peter Burakoff
Artwork by Elizabeth Jensen
Printed in Canada by Friesen Printers
Front & Back Cover Photos: David Hancock

Hancock House Publishers
256 Route 81, Killingworth, CT, U.S.A. 06417
Hancock House Publishers Ltd.
19313 Zero Avenue, Surrey, B.C., Canada V3S 5J9

Table of Contents

Acknowledgment 7
1. About Shellfishing 8
2. Clams 12
3. Oysters... 28
4. Scallops 34
5. Blue Mussels....................................... 40
6. Keeping and Cleaning Your Catch 44
7. Cooking Your Catch 55

Acknowledgment

Special thanks are due to Dana Rowan, who did much of the research and contributed to the writing of this book.

Secrets of Shellfishing

Whether you are a veteran beachcomber, a vacationer seeking new adventures, or simply a lover of fresh seafood, gathering your own shellfish is both fun and, with a little foresight, rather easy. You don't need a boat for most shellfishing, and, unlike the equipment for other types of fishing, the equipment for shellfishing is simple and inexpensive. The rewards, moreover, are great, because shellfish are truly gourmet treats.

Shellfishing is one of the oldest forms of hunting. Shell fragments in primitive cave dwellings show that shellfish were a staple for many prehistoric people. Along the coasts of North America, centuries-old mounds of shell fragments testify that shellfishing is an ancient American tradition. These mounds were built up over the years as the Indians gathered shellfish, removed the delicious meat, and tossed the shells onto a trash heap.

European colonists brought their own shellfishing skills to America. Like the Indians, early seaboard colonists depended on shellfish as a source of food. Later, shellfishing became a major industry, supporting large companies as well as individual fishermen. It employed thousands of fishermen and people in processing plants, and made millionaires out of some aggressive businessmen.

The industry still thrives today, but shellfishing has also become a favorite recreational pursuit of many people who live near or visit the sea. Most coastal states promote shellfishing but also regulate it. Regulation is necessary both to conserve this precious resource and to prevent people from eating shellfish contaminated by disease or pollution.

The careful shellfish gatherer can enjoy harvests without fear, but the careless fisherman runs considerable risk. Red tide, the natural contamination of the water by a sudden population explosion of microscopic creatures named dinoflagellates, can poison shellfish. Red tides occur frequently in some areas and hardly ever in others, but they always are closely monitored by health and conservation authorities. *Never* take shellfish from an area where red tide is even suspected.

Sewage, chemical wastes, and other pollution will contaminate shellfish. Sometimes the shellfish themselves will be killed, but sometimes they will accumulate viruses or poisons that will harm anyone who eats them. Hepatitis, a serious disease that affects the liver, can be contracted by eating shellfish that have been exposed to contaminated sewage. The viruses that cause hepatitis become concentrated in the shellfish and are ingested by the diner. Several other ailments can also be contracted by eating contaminated shellfish.

This knowledge should make you cautious, but it should not discourage you. A simple safety rule is never eat shellfish from an area you do not know is absolutely safe. And don't take just anyone's word for it. Make sure it's official. Signs warning people that shellfish in a particular place are dangerous are often posted on utility poles and fences, but don't assume everything is safe just because you cannot find a sign. Check with the appropriate authority first. Most municipalities that have shellfish abundant within their boundaries have a shellfish commission that monitors the quality of the shellfish. The commission can tell you where it is safe to take shellfish and whether or not you need a license to do so. Usually licenses cost only a few dollars. If there is no shellfish commission in the area, check with your state conservation or marine agency, or contact the state health department.

1. CLAMS

Clams are among the world's most delectable shellfish. They can be served in a variety of ways, including raw, baked, or in chowder. The types of clams most often eaten are found in the area between the high-tide mark and the 60-foot mark in sheltered bays, coves, or inlets that have mud, sand, or clay bottoms. The key requirement for the survival of clams is salinity. They do not flourish in water that contains less than 15 parts of salt per thousand of water. Oceanic sea water is about 35 parts salt. The salinity decreases in estuaries, but most estuarine environments except those at the mouths of large rivers will have water salty enough to support clam beds.

The Hard-shell Clam

The hard-shell clam, also known as the quahog, ranges the Atlantic Coast from Canada's Gulf of St. Lawrence to Florida. Its favorite habitat is shallow backwaters in quiet, sheltered bays and coves. This clam can be found on bottoms of several types, including gravel, mud, and sand, but is most abundant where mud and sand mix. The best level of salinity for hard clams is between 18 and 26 parts per thousand, although they can tolerate water that is more or less salty.

Hard clams eat small organisms that are in the water. The clam uses its gills to create currents that force the water bearing the food towards its siphon. The water flows into the siphon and the organisms are caught in the gills, then transferred to the clam's mouth and swallowed. The water is then expelled through another siphon.

Sometimes sand is caught in the gills and may irritate the clam. The sand passes to the base of the siphon and is eventually forced out with water. When preparing clams for the table, or eating them raw, wash the body parts to remove sand that is building up near the siphon.

Clams become sexually mature in two to four years and may switch sex from one year to the next. Spawning may begin as soon as the water has warmed up, and usually takes place from late spring to midsummer, though mostly in summer. A single female clam may produce up to twenty-four million eggs in one spawning. Fertilization takes place in the water. Once they hatch, young clams go through several stages as larvae, which look quite different from the adults we eat. Within two weeks, however, the clam settles to the bottom and anchors there by means of a mass of threads called a byssus. The byssus attaches to grains of sand and similar small objects. Before long, the larval clam is buried in sand and sediment. Its body begins to change and a siphon is formed, which pokes through the sand into the water. A shell begins to develop and after a month or so the clam assumes the adult form that graces our tables, although it is still very small.

As they grow, hard clams are known by three different names according to size. The big adults, which are tougher and slightly less sweet than smaller ones, are known as *chowder clams*, because they are usually cooked in soup. They are also good stuffed or ground up for clam fritters. *Cherrystone clams* are medium-sized, often eaten raw on the halfshell or served baked. *Little necks* are the smallest and sweetest and are mostly eaten raw on the halfshell.

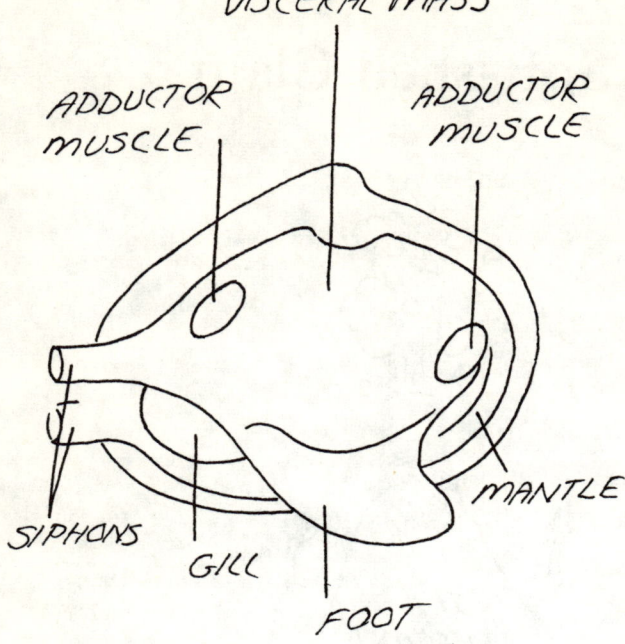

SOFT PARTS OF A BIVALVE

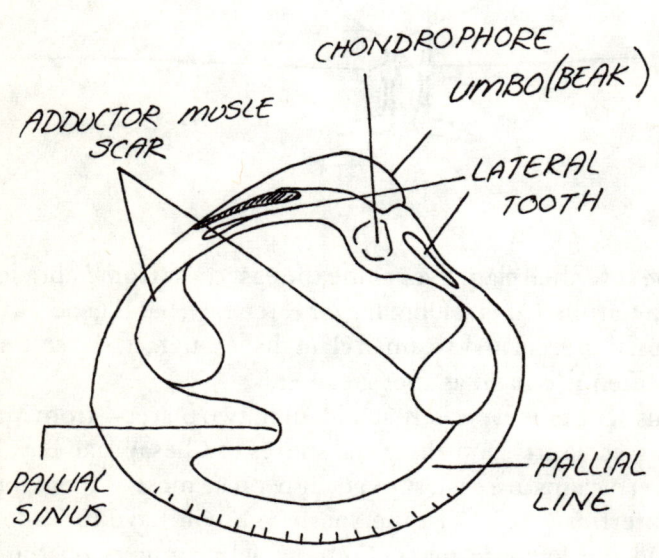

SHELL INTERIOR

The Soft-shell Clam

The soft-shell clam lives along the east coast from Labrador to North Carolina. It is seldom if ever eaten raw, but is generally the type used in fried and steamed clam dishes. In fact, the soft-shell clam often is known as the "steamer."

This species is especially abundant in two places—from Maine to Massachusetts, and along the shores of Chesapeake Bay. The northern clams are easiest to get at because most of them live in the intertidal region. In the south, you will have to wade out beyond the low-tide mark. Commercial clammers on the Bay dredge clams from boats.

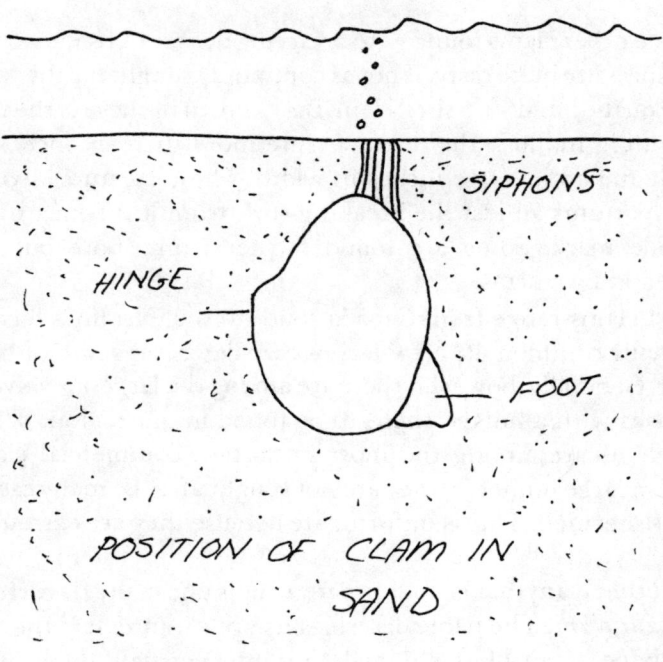

Soft-shell clams spawn between June and August in Maine, from July to September along the coast of Massachusetts north of Cape Cod, and twice yearly to the south. Along the Chesapeake, the clams reproduce in May and June and then again in September and October.

The larvae are free swimming at first but then settle to the bottom, attaching by threads. The attachment is temporary. The young clam sometimes moves about on its single foot or is carried by currents. When it is about an inch long, however, it digs a burrow that will be its permanent home. The clam excavates as it grows. Under favorable conditions, a soft-shell clam can reach two inches in less than two years.

Soft-shell clams feed a variety of other beachcombers besides humans. Green crabs like them. So do drills, horseshoe crabs, sea gulls, ducks, and flounders. Cow-nosed rays also cruise the bottom looking for these clams to eat.

Other Clams

Some other clams found with a varying degree of frequency on our shores are quite tasty, if not as commonly sought for the table as the quahog and soft-shell clam. Best known of these is the *surf clam*, a big mollusk that can measure more than six inches in length and almost five inches in width. These creatures live in sandy bottoms amidst the breaking surf, from just beneath the low-tide mark. Some are found farther from shore but are washed in by storms.

Surf clams range from Canada south to the Carolinas but are especially common off New Jersey. Size decreases south of New Jersey. Generally, however, these are among the largest bivalves—mollusks with a hinged shell—to be found in our region. While surf clams are among the most important commercial clams taken in large numbers, they are not sought after by many casual clam fishermen. This is unfortunate because they are extremely tasty.

Another clam that is seldom eaten but is unusually flavorful is the *razor clam*. The name describes its appearance. It is the size and shape of an old-fashioned straight razor, although older individuals sometimes get larger, occasionally approaching a foot in length.

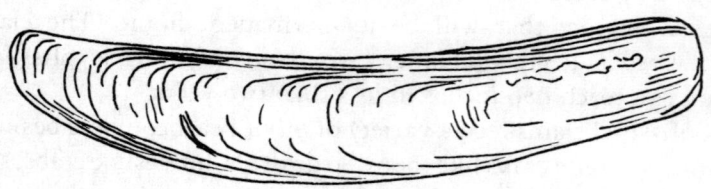

The razor clam ranges from Canada to the Carolinas and prefers to live just below the low-tide mark in sandy-bottomed areas. It has a very strong, long foot that slices down into the sand, allowing the thin, elongate shell of the clam to slip neatly into the sand like a letter-opener into an envelope. The clam is an extremely fast digger, able to bury itself in a few seconds. This adaptation enables the razor clam to survive under the pounding of the surf.

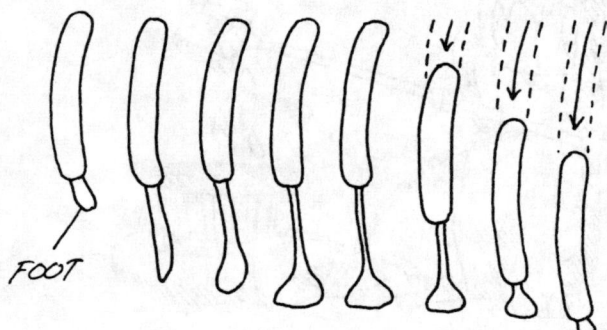

HOW A RAZOR CLAM DIGS

FOOT

MUSCLES FORCE WATER INTO FOOT, FOOT SPREADS OUT, ACTS AS "ANCHOR" OTHER MUSCLES ARE THEN USED TO PULL CLAM DOWN TOWARDS "ANCHOR"

Clamming from Shore

You can get plenty of clams from the shore without a boat. A method called "scratching" for clams works well in the inshore shallows. Standard equipment for this method includes a pair of sneakers or hip boots for wading—these, of course, are useful for all sorts of clamming where wading is required—plus a bucket or basket fitted with an inner tube and tied to your waist, and a tool known as a "scratcher."

The bucket is for holding the clams you find. The scratcher is for finding them. It is a long-handled, six-tined digging tool that looks like a garden rake with a basket attached behind the head.

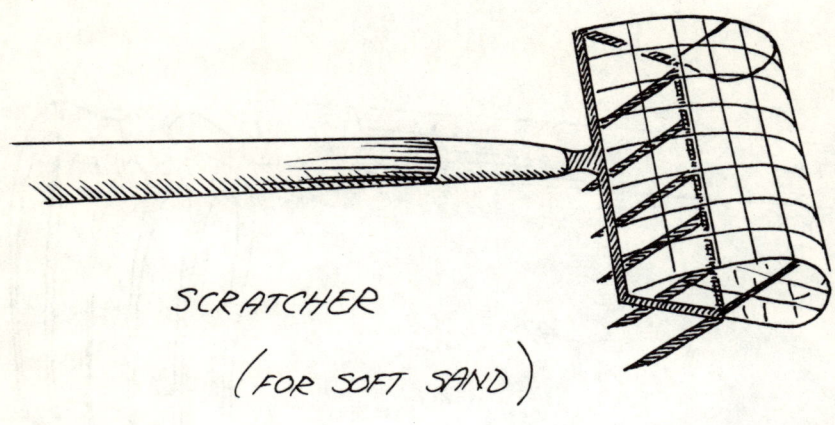

SCRATCHER (FOR SOFT SAND)

As the tines dig up the clams, they are caught and held in the basket. To use the scratcher, extend it fully in front of you and then work it towards you, as if loosening up soil in the garden. As you scratch, the clams will be pulled into the basket.

Scratching with a basket is best done in shallow water at low tide on intertidal flats. The lower the tide the better, because it leaves you more time to work. The flats have the most clams, but they are covered by the incoming tide before areas higher in the intertidal zone. Thus, work the flats first, then move inshore as the water advances. Also, remember that the basket scratcher works best in soft sand, not bottoms that are rock strewn or hard.

If you are confronted with bottoms that are rocky or fouled with shells or other debris, try "turfing." The tool for this technique is a clam hoe, also called a "clam rake," or "claw rake." Clam hoes have tines about a foot long, numbering between four and eight, depending on the type or model. The number and style of the tines depends on the bottom. For example, use a four-tined hoe with long, wide tines in wet, soupy sand or light mud. In clayey mud or tightly packed sand use a hoe with narrower, shorter, and more widely spaced tines.

It's tough to find a good clam hoe, so you may prefer to make your own. Buy a style of pitchfork that most closely suits your needs and take it to a garage that has an acetylene torch. Have the

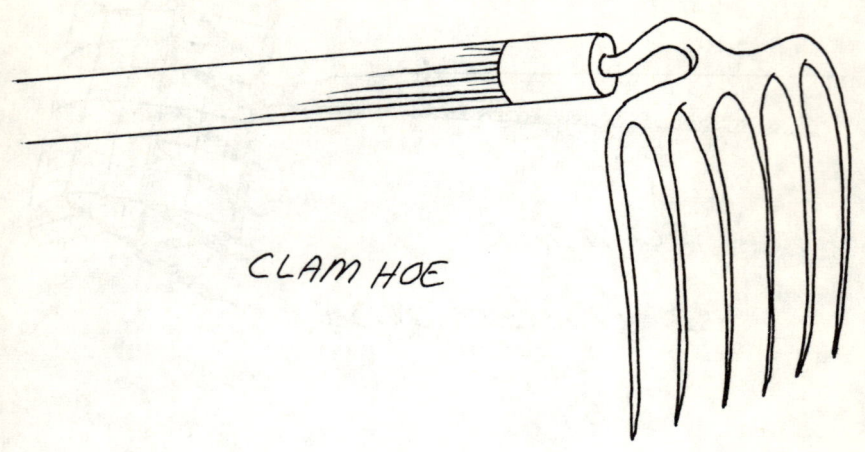

CLAM HOE

A GOOD CLAM HOE FOR GRAVEL

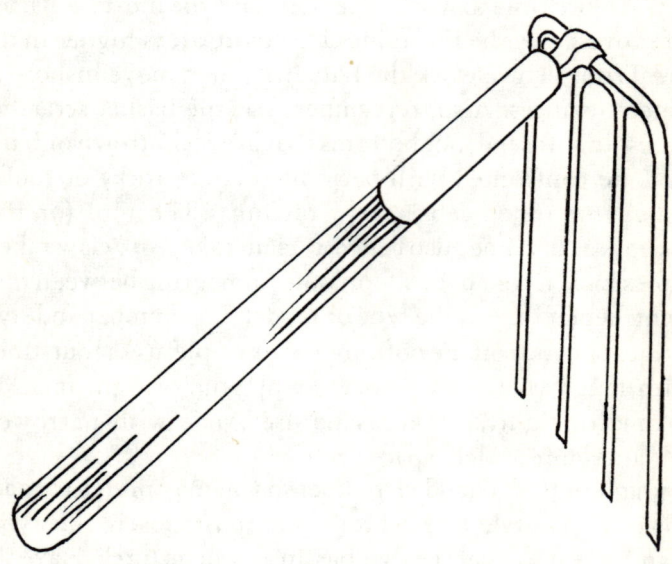

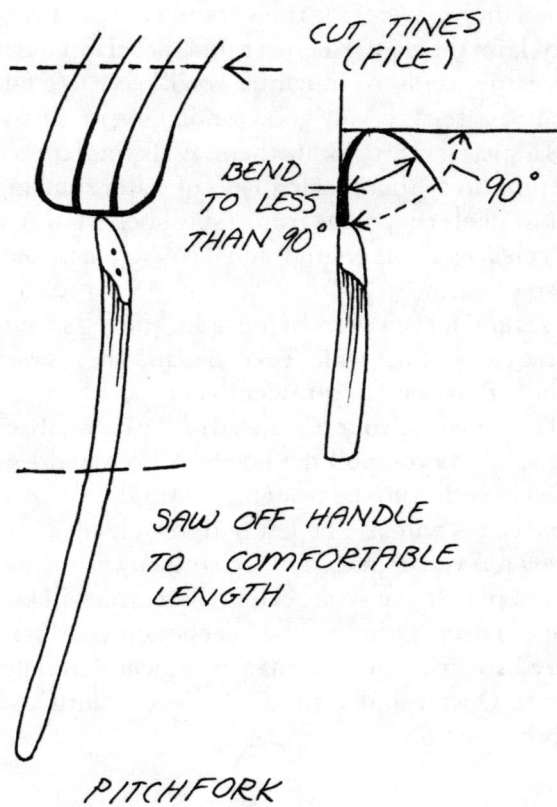

PITCHFORK

tines bent so that they are at slightly less than ninety degrees (a right angle) to the handle. Saw off the handle to a comfortable length, grind or hacksaw the points of the tines (make them flat, not narrow), and be careful not to draw the temper out of the steel by filing it when too hot. Now you are ready to "turf."

Turfing works this way. Dig a hole three inches deep and three or four times the diameter of your hoe. Thrust the hoe's tines firmly into the bottom sediment six inches in front of the hole and pull hard on the hoe. The sediment should be pulled backward into the hole, exposing beds of clams that were hidden beneath it.

You can also use the hoe to drag through the bottom. When it strikes a clam you'll feel the tines bounce over it. Back up and dig down to claim the clam. Keep in mind that clams burrow further as the weather cools, so in winter you'll have to go deep.

Clam hoes are especially good for digging up soft-shell clams. There is a special way to locate them. Walk the exposed intertidal flat, keeping an eye out for small jets of water spurting out of the sand; most likely they come from a soft-shell clam. You may find the squirt leaves a hole behind, and if you're lucky you'll see more in a cluster nearby.

Start several feet away from the holes and dig a trough that's at least three to four hoes wide. Take the sand out in layers until you have a hole that you are confident is deeper than the burrowed clams. Then, placing your hoe ahead of the holes, thrust the tines into the sand. As you pull the hoe back evenly, the sand should topple backwards into the trough, bottom side up. And if you are lucky, the clams will also be left bottom side up.

However, if you do not come up with any clams, sort through the discard pile. If you strike clams there, you will know you are working too deep. Otherwise, go deeper on your next try. Most good-sized steamers (larger than two inches) should be on the same level. Once you determine the level, continue to work at that depth.

If you work intertidal areas when they are still covered with water, and it is warm, "treading" can be a productive method of collecting clams. Treading is done by wading out to where you think the clams are and feeling around the bottom with your feet. Don't try it barefooted—you might be cut by a sharp shell. Even with tennis shoes, or the rubber booties used by skin divers, you'll have enough sensitivity to feel the clams by foot. Once you find them, reach down and work after them with your fingers or a rake.

"Holing" clams is a search technique that depends on having sharp eyes. Buried clams are revealed by the holes through which they protrude their siphons. When it is high tide and the bottom is covered by water, the siphons are up and operating. At low tide they are withdrawn, and the holes are partly filled, but visible. On dry, flat sand, the holes may look like splattered drops, as though someone has splashed a ladle of water hard across the sand. In hard, dark mud, look for marks of similar shape and size, but surrounded by a light circle. Wherever you see holes, there probably are clams below. Go after them with a hoe or even a plain old garden pitchfork. Dig quickly and chances are you'll catch them.

Clamming from a Boat

If you have the use of a boat you can reach clams not accessible by wading. Make sure the boat is stable, with a high sturdy beam that will enable you to lean over it and work without falling out.

"Tonging" is one way of clamming from a boat. It gets its name from the tool that is used, which looks like a pair of oversized kitchen tongs with wooden handles. The business end of the tongs has a pair of heads in the form of half-baskets tipped by short, sharp teeth. When the tongs are dug into the bottom and brought together, they scoop up the clams along with the sediment, which slips through the openings in the basket, leaving only the clams. Tongs are best used in soft bottoms.

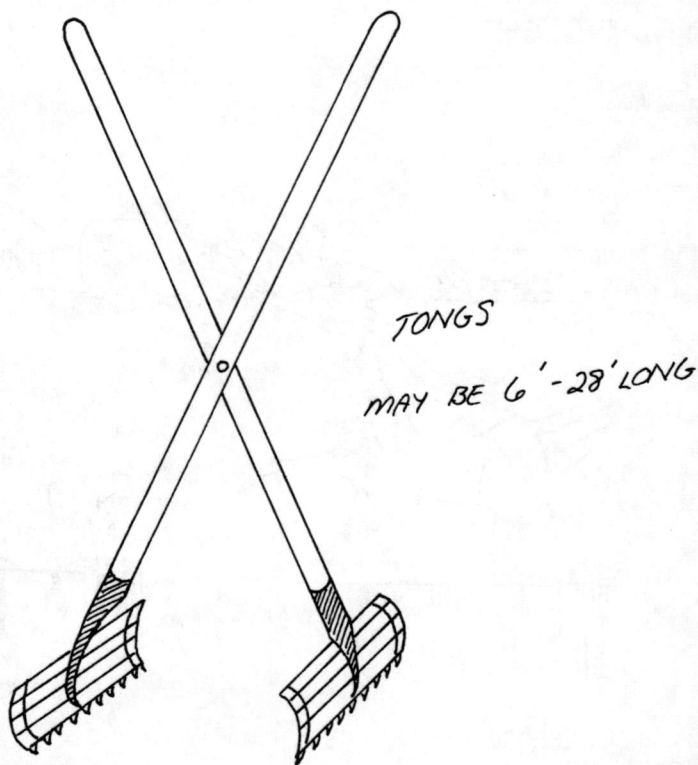

TONGS MAY BE 6'-28' LONG

Tongs come in different lengths; the one you use depends on the depth of the water in which you are operating. Most tongs are between three and twelve feet in length, although some are up to twenty-five feet in length. The longer tongs are not for beginners, as they are very difficult to wield.

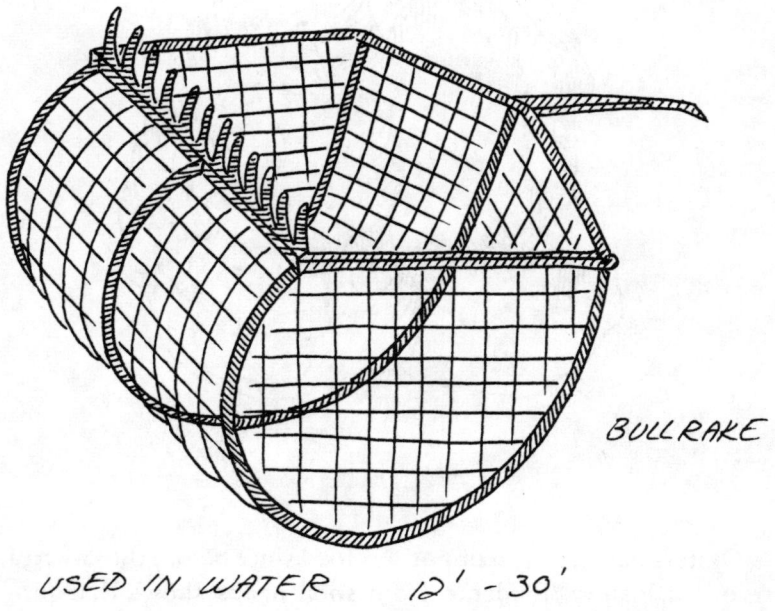

BULLRAKE

USED IN WATER 12' - 30'

Raking involves using long, heavy rakes from the boat, and it requires practice. The bull rake has a heavy, solid head with a row of markedly curved tines. It must be very sturdy. The handle can range from a dozen feet to more than thirty feet. Sea stories tell of old-timers who used rakes almost a hundred feet long. To use the rake, put the head on the bottom and drag it through the sediment. The head should be heavy enough to dig in on its own when you pull it. You should not have to press down. The idea is to catch clams in the crook of the tines. Once you think you have some, stand up, hold the rake with the handle pointing skyward, and pull it up at right angles to the bottom so the clams do not fall out.

2. OYSTERS

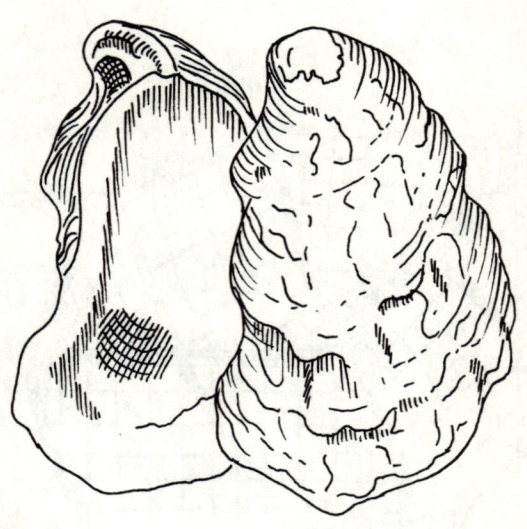

Oysters have been an important food since before the dawn of recorded history. Evidence from shell heaps shows that prehistoric people who lived by the seaside ate them regularly. Because oysters grow along most of the world's coasts, many cultures made use of them. The Romans, for instance, featured oysters at their lavish feasts. Favorite oystering grounds for the Romans were the shores of Brittany and Britain.

When Europeans came to America they also utilized the plentiful oyster beds they found along the Atlantic coast. So important to the colonists was the oyster that it was the subject of some of their first laws, which regulated the harvest and the types of implements that could be used.

Oysters grow in beds that are easy to see and close to shore, although not always accessible without a boat. The oyster is a true creature of brackish estuarine waters, which is one reason it is so

abundant in places such as Chesapeake Bay. Oysters tolerate much lower salinity—down to five parts salt per thousand of water—than clams.

The oyster has a soft body enclosed by two hinged shells. If you look closely, you will find that the body lies in one shell, always the one that is cupped most deeply. Within the body are the oyster's organs, nervous system, and circulatory system. All are enfolded by a structure called a mantle, typical of mollusks, containing glands that secrete shell-building material. As the oyster grows, the mantle continues to build up the shell, which gets larger with age. Oysters reach adult size in two to four years. Strong muscles called adductors are attached to the shells of the oysters and control their opening and closing.

Gills not only allow the oyster to breathe but also enable it to eat. They filter out bits of food from the water that the oyster pumps through them. The food then goes to the digestive tract.

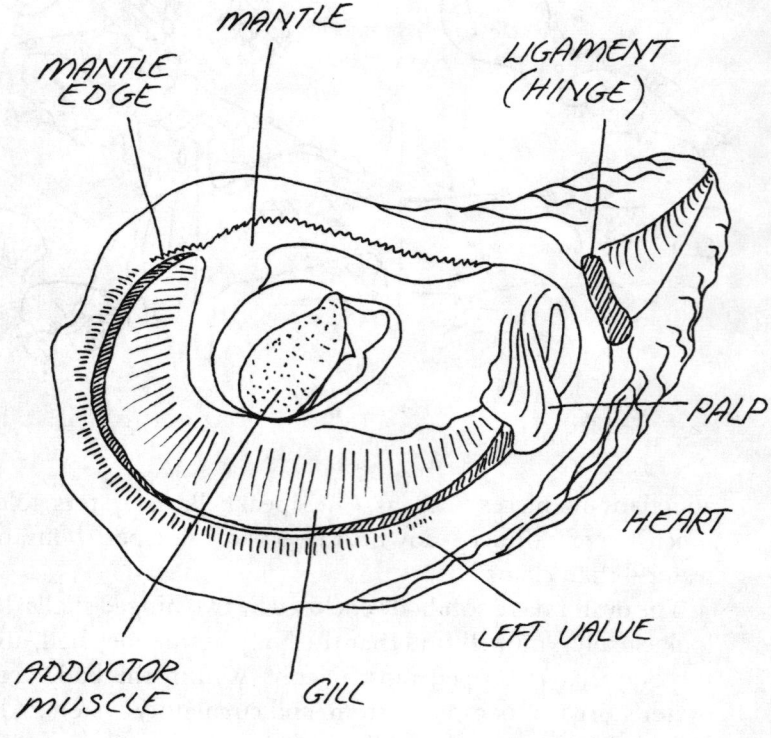

The majority of oysters start life as males and remain so until after the first time they spawn. Many of them then change sex. The ratio of males to females will be about equal by the second spawning.

Oysters spawn when the temperature of the water is about 74°F. The eggs and sperm are shed and float in the water, where they unite. The larvae that result are not attached organisms, like the adults, but swim freely. In about two weeks, however, they settle to the bottom and attach themselves to rocks and other smooth, hard objects. At this stage they are called "spat." From this point on the oysters, which already have small shells, start growing toward adult size.

One of the favorite places for spat to settle is on old oyster shells. Spat look like tiny, light brown specks, about the size of a pinhead, on the surface of the shells. The tendency for spat to take up residence on old shells is precisely what creates oyster beds. Many beds are 90 percent old shells and 10 percent live oysters. From the Carolinas north, most oysters grow in places that are covered with water throughout the entire tidal cycle. This makes them more difficult to get at than clams. However, you can often find them in water shallow enough to wade in, or at least close enough to shore so you only need a small boat to get there.

The best time to harvest oysters is in the cooler months. Oysters generally spawn in June, and that makes them thin and watery throughout the summer. In addition, regulations in many eastern states prohibit the collection of oysters during the summer months.

If you plan to eat your oysters on the halfshell, be particular about taste and quality. Gourmets prefer salty oysters, complaining that an unsalty oyster is bland and too fishy. Keep this in mind when you map out your areas to hunt--salty water makes a salty oyster, so avoid the river mouth or creek-fed bay.

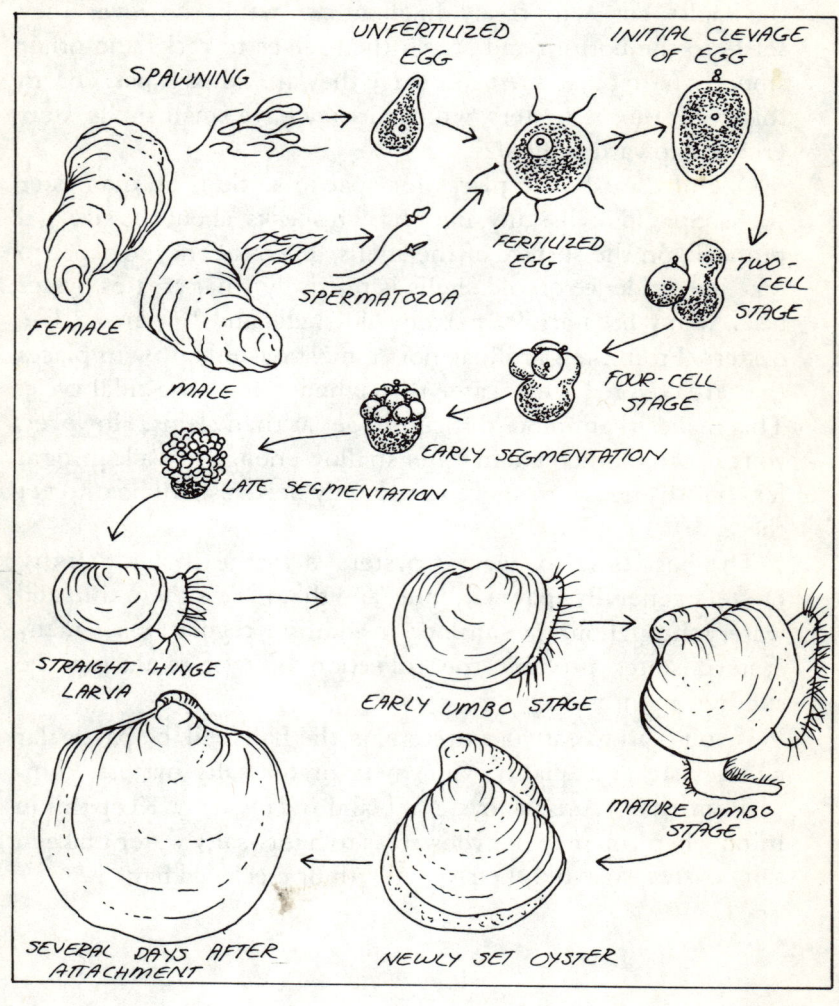

Easy Oystering

Oyster beds are often found on shallow, irregular bars. Once you have located a productive bed, approach it carefully. Oysters are irregular, brittle, and, most importantly, razor sharp. Be sure you wear a durable pair of sneakers and, if necessary, a pair of cloth or cowhide work gloves. Using a wooden mallet, a piece of pipe, or a two-by-four, strike the bed and free the oysters. You will find that most of the shells are literally cemented together and malformed, so it may take a bit of effort. Chances are the animals will break off in clusters. Rather than try to separate them out in the water, stow them in your sack or wire basket and haul them back to the beach.

Once back on the beach, you may find a large flat piece of driftwood useful as a pounding table. Separate the oysters and wash them with a scrub brush. Then they are ready to take home.

"Clamming" for Oysters

Most of the methods described for clamming from a boat can be used to obtain oysters beyond the shallows. If you can get a boat out over an oyster bed in deeper water, you can use tongs to pry them loose and haul them to the surface. It is more difficult and takes more muscle than tonging for clams. However, tonging enables you to get at oysters you might otherwise miss. A bull rake also comes in handy for bringing up oysters from way down below. Use it for oysters just as you do for clams. Don't try to use force; let the weight of the rake carry it into the massed oysters, and with luck it will come up laden.

3. SCALLOPS

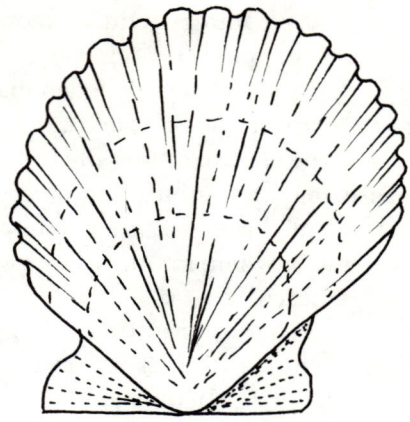

The bay scallop, also known as the Cape Cod scallop, is one of the most prized bivalves, though its meat has not always been appreciated. In the eighteenth century and most of the nineteenth century, Americans regarded the scallop as a poisonous organism, unfit for the table. The only thing early Americans admired was its beautiful, highly colored shell. Needless to say, times have changed. Today most scallops don't live beyond two years—the average time required for the animal to reach harvestable size, more than two inches in diameter.

Scallops are found from Maine to North Carolina. Unfortunately, they are extremely sensitive to pollution, and with the large increase in coastal development they have become difficult to find.

In this country, most of the scallop's body is discarded during preparation. Only the large adductor muscle is eaten. This muscle is used to propel the scallop, so it is much more developed than in other bivalves.

Scallops are actually quite mobile. Unlike the clam or oyster, scallops don't rely on the slow, methodical pace of a muscular foot. Instead, the animal's adductor muscle clamps the shell shut in a single motion, releasing a jet of water that the scallop can direct. This action shoots the bivalve through the water and, if repeated in rapid series, can quickly move the scallop a considerable distance.

The scallop's sensory system is also more sophisticated than that of most other members of the mollusk family. The animal detects motion and changes in light intensity using a series of light sensors that project from the edge of the mantle. These can trigger the reflex contractions of the animal's adductor muscle in an effort to escape predators. The combination of this system with its mobility makes a scallop more of a challenge to catch than other bivalves.

The animal spawns, using external fertilization, from June through August, and prefers subtidal habitat out to about twenty-five feet of water. Along the east coast, the harvest season commonly lasts from October through March.

Catching Scallops

There are basically three simple ways to catch scallops for the table, and all work best with a boat. You don't need a fancy skiff, just a simple flat-bottomed rowboat. These methods are ideal for shallow water (knee deep at low tide) particularly in areas where the bottom is covered with eel grass. Incidentally, because this plant is sensitive to pollution, its presence indicates a healthy environment for scallops.

Whatever method you use, first scan the water from the rowboat looking for eel grass beds. Once you have located and rowed to them, step out of the rowboat--remember to wear hip boots or sneakers—leaving the boat upwind of the grounds you plan to work. The boat will act as a wind spoil to smooth out the surface water interference so you can see the bottom and the scallops clearly.

The only equipment you need for the method called dip netting is a simple, light dip net to snag the scallops and something to hold them until you are ready to return to the boat. A dip net looks like a butterfly net but is sturdier. It should be about eight inches in diameter and have a handle a yard or more long. Dip nets can be bought in most areas where scalloping is good. For holding your catch, a net diving bag—you can find one at almost any dive shop—is good. You also can use a fisherman's net bag, the kind that is tied over the side of a boat to hold small fish and keep them alive after they have been caught.

Netting scallops is real sport, because the creatures are so active and mobile. The technique is to wade slowly, taking care to disturb the water as little as possible, and scoop up the scallops as soon as you see them. It is not as easy as it sounds, but it is lots of fun.

The dip net has one drawback, however: its rim is round. When scooped along the bottom, the round shape allows space between the net and the bottom for scallops to escape.

A different net design favored years ago but not used widely today, is the push net. The leading edge of the push net is flat and

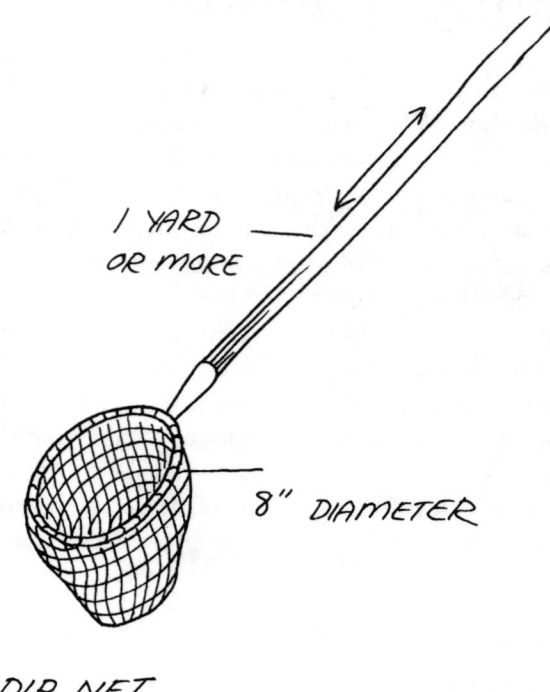

DIP NET

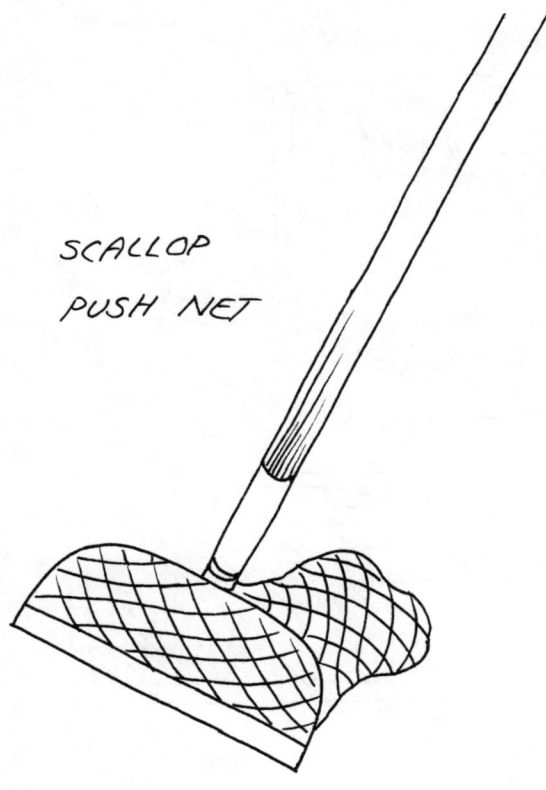

fitted with an inch-wide flat piece of iron. You can use the push net like a dip net, or sweep it along the bottom. Since it is flush with the bottom, the scallops have less chance to escape. This technique, for obvious reasons, is called "push netting."

Perhaps the most popular way of catching scallops is to use a device known as a "looking box." It can only be used from a boat. The looking box serves the same purpose as the glass-fronted mask of a skin diver. It enables you to see clearly in the water, without distortion. The box is open on top, with a bottom of clear glass ten inches by twelve inches enclosed on four sides with wood panels—marine plywood is best. The box must be watertight, so you should line the seams with a good caulking material. As an option, you can tack a cloth along the top rim of the box to reduce the glare of the sun. You may also want to put a strap on the box so you can fasten it round your neck when you are using it, a safeguard against its falling into the water.

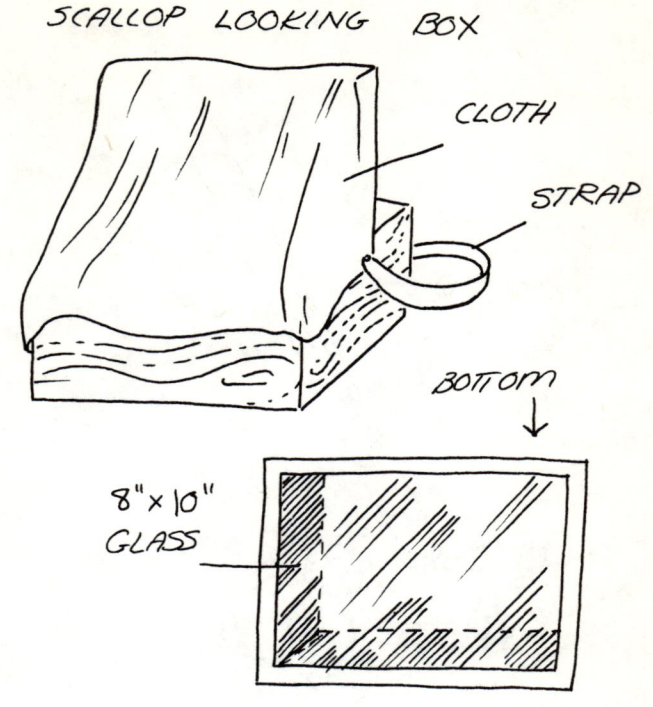
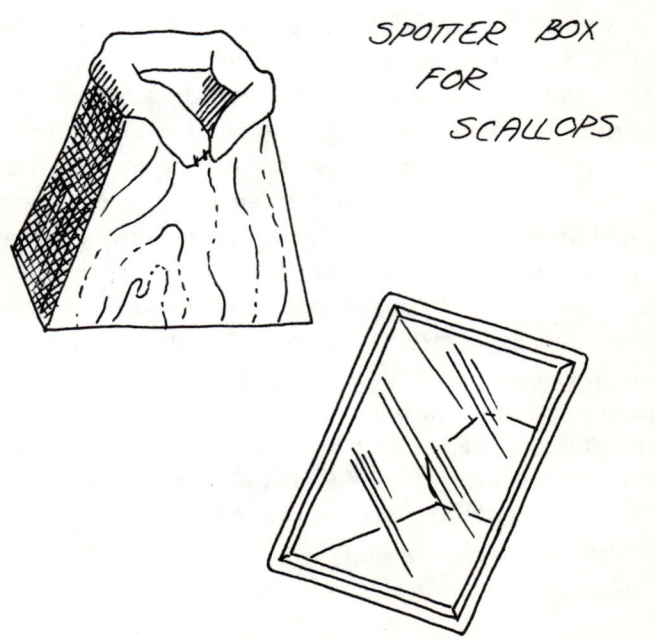

As your boat drifts over a scallop bed, lean over the side, holding the box in one hand—this is why a strap is a good idea—with the glass bottom submerged. Look through the glass for scallops. Have a dip net or push net in the other hand, ready for action. Once you master the technique it is at least as productive as wading, with the added benefit of enabling you to work in deeper water. A wire fish basket or wooden bushel basket aboard the boat will serve well to hold the scallops you catch.

4. BLUE MUSSELS

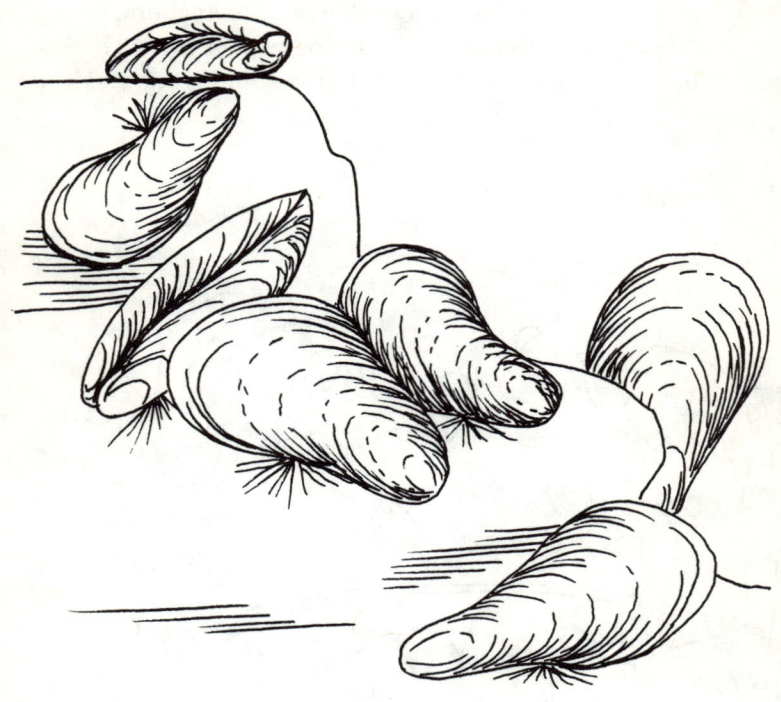

The blue mussel is more commonly seen along most of the coast than clams, oyster, or scallops. It attaches to pilings, rocks, and other surfaces, mostly in the intertidal zone. Some parts of the intertidal zone are so thick with mussels you cannot even see the rocks. In Europe, and among Americans whose ancestors come from countries such as Italy, Spain, and France, mussels are considered among the finest of seafoods. Yet they are not big sellers in most United States fish markets; nor are they harvested for the table with anything near the frequency of similar shellfish. And this is unfortunate, because properly cooked mussels are delicious.

So delicate are mussels in taste, in fact, that Europeans call them the "poor man's oyster." Surveys of American consumers who have broken with custom and tried mussels show that to the palate of many people, mussels taste better than clams, are rich and robust, and have a hint of an oyster flavor.

As a food, mussels rate high in nutrition. They have more nutrient value per pound of shucked meat than most other shellfish, including lobster, clams, and oysters. Even more surprising is that mussels contain more protein per pound than choice beef. The mussel industry had its only real boom here during World War II, when there was a worldwide shortage of meat protein. Because mussels were an unfamiliar food in this country, however, most of those harvested during the war were shipped overseas.

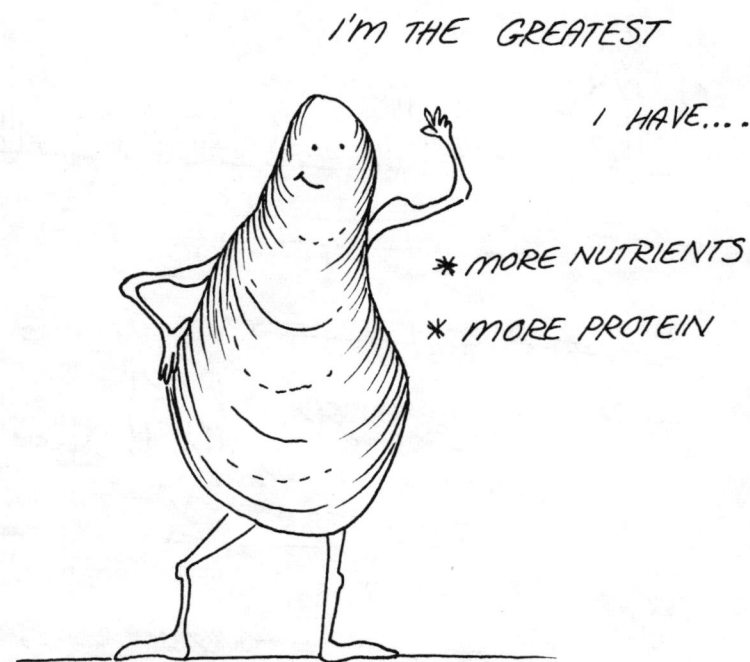

The blue mussel is between two and three inches long when adult, with a shell that is violet-blue on the outside, but often covered with a darker, blacker material. Inside, the shell is pearl colored, outlined by dark blue. The soft body parts are vivid orange. The mussel attaches itself to a surface by producing threads called a byssus from glands in the foot. Mussels live in extremely dense, close-packed colonies, with one layer of the animals building up on the other. Sometimes the mussels jam together so tightly that they lose their anchors, begin to buckle, and are eventually torn away by the surf.

Blue mussels are very tolerant of tidal conditions and can remain out of water for long periods of the day. They are also very adaptable to different types of habitat, being found on anything from rocks and coarse sand to silty mud. Among their natural constraints are high water temperatures, low salinity, poor water circulation, and really heavy surf. For these reasons, you won't find them south of the Carolinas, in places where freshwater rivers enter the sea, or where there is very heavy wave action.

Harvesting Mussels

It is easier to harvest mussels than clams, oysters, or scallops. Look for mussels at low tide when the beds are exposed. Often you will not even have to wade to get at them. And once you find them, you probably will have all you want in one place—that's how crowded the beds are. Fancy tools are unnecessary. You can use a rake, a garden cultivator, a clam scratcher, or even just your hands, though you should wear gloves. Simply pull or claw the mussels upward and off their place of attachment. Put them in a bucket or similar receptacle. They are ready for cleaning and preparation.

5. KEEPING AND CLEANING YOUR CATCH

A Word of Warning

If a harvested shellfish has its shells parted, leave it alone. Chances are it is dead or unhealthy. You don't want to risk getting sick by eating it.

Hard-shell Clams

Hard-shell clams can be kept at least overnight in a refrigerator. Once you are ready to eat them, they require little cleaning. Run them under cold, fresh water, scrubbing off any dirt.

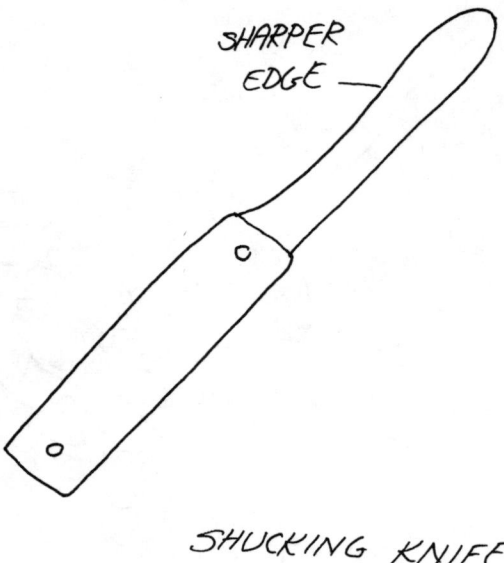

SHUCKING KNIFE

Opening, or "shucking," clams takes some practise. The tool can be any small knife, but it is best to use one designed for the purpose. The shucking knife has a finger-long blade with a wooden handle of about the same length. The blade is flat and thin, but not sharp, eliminating the danger of cutting yourself if the knife happens to slip.

The following instructions for opening are for right-handed people. If you are a lefty, reverse the procedure.

Pick up the clam in your left hand, knife in the right. Work one edge of the knife into the tiny space between the shells. As soon as the knife penetrates, slide it back and forth from one end of the rim to the other, cutting the muscle that holds the shells fast. Open up the shell and rinse off the clam's soft parts to remove sand.

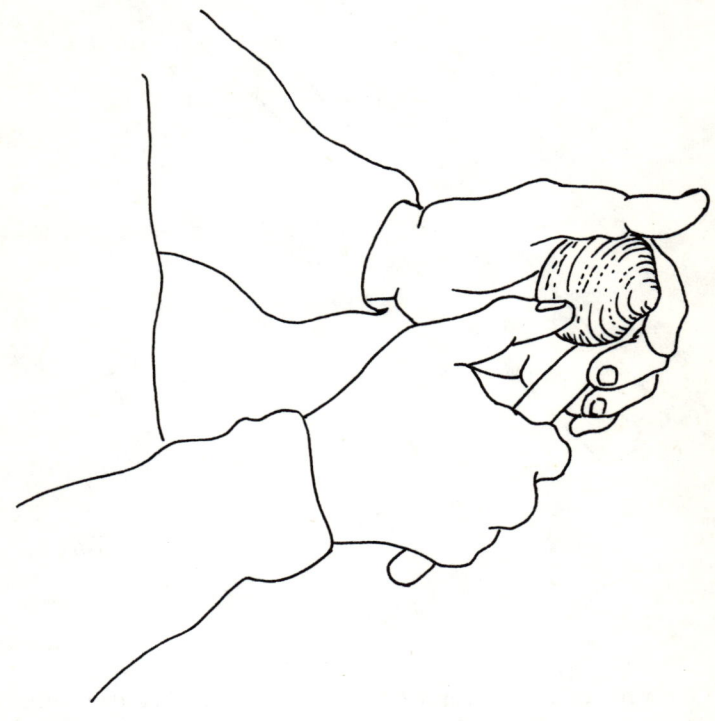

To open, hold clam in your left hand and knife in your right hand.

If you have trouble getting the knife in, try the following trick. Drop the clams into a pot holding a few inches of water and heat it. The heat will make the clams open up enough for you to insert the knife easily. This technique can be used with similar shellfish as well.

Razor Clams and Surf Clams

Treat razor and surf clams just as you do hard-shells. But be careful not to cut yourself on the razor clam's shell: as its name implies, the edges are sharp.

Soft-shell Clams

Soft-shell clams should be used quickly. They will not last more than a day or so in the refrigerator. There is no need to open soft-shells while they are alive because they are used in recipes that call for cooking them first. Take care to clean soft-shells well, however, because they are usually covered with sediment outside and often have it inside as well. Scrub the outside of the shells under the cold water tap. Sometimes this is all you need to do. But if the clams have a large amount of sediment inside, you will have to purge them—or, rather, permit them to do it themselves.

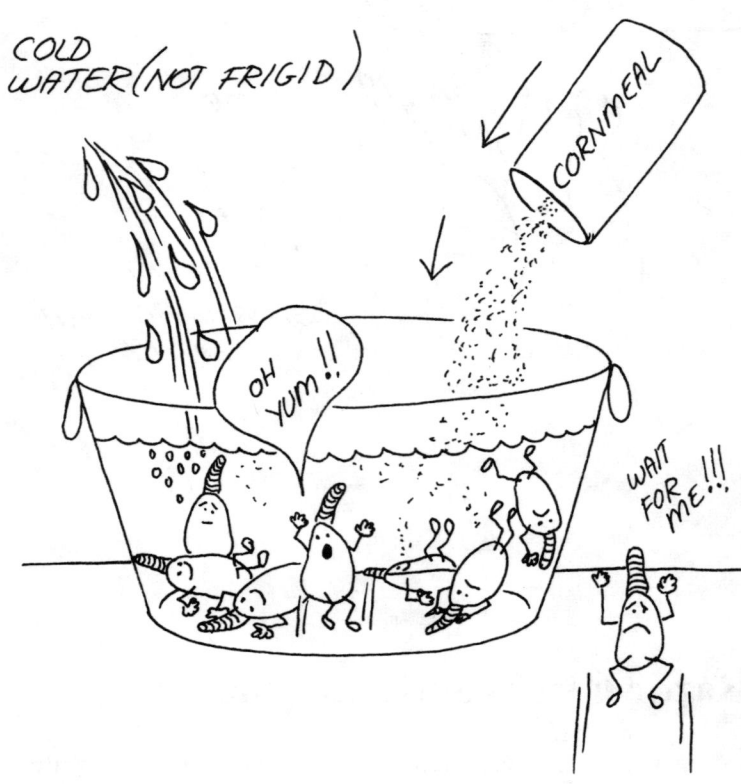

To purge soft-shells, place them in a sink or bucket, leaving them strewn around rather than piled one on top of the other. Cover them with cold, but not frigid, water. Sprinkle some cornmeal into the water. The clams will ingest the cornmeal, then flush it out, and with it the dirt that was inside them. Leave the clams in the water for a day before preparing them. Recipes for cooking the clams will be given later. For now, however, remember that once the soft-shells are cooked, the shells will open and you can remove the meat by hand. To clean, pull off the sock-like, blackish mantle that encases the siphon. Then add them to whatever dish you are making.

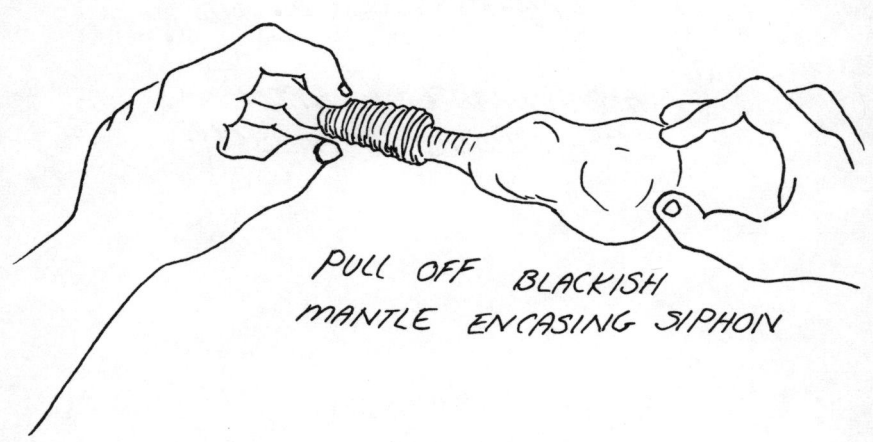

PULL OFF BLACKISH MANTLE ENCASING SIPHON

Oysters

Oysters should be scrubbed to remove dirt from the outside of their shells. That is easy—but opening them is not. The traditional way to open oysters is to work your knife edge between the shells, while holding the oyster from its hinged side.

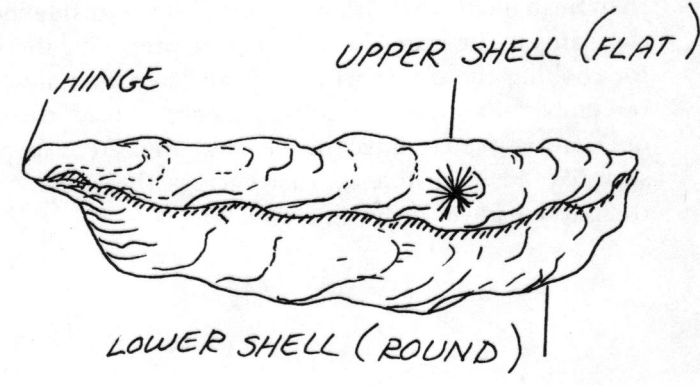

OYSTER (SIDE VIEW)

HINGE
UPPER SHELL (FLAT)
LOWER SHELL (ROUND)

✳ APPROXIMATE LOCATION OF ADDUCTOR MUSCLE

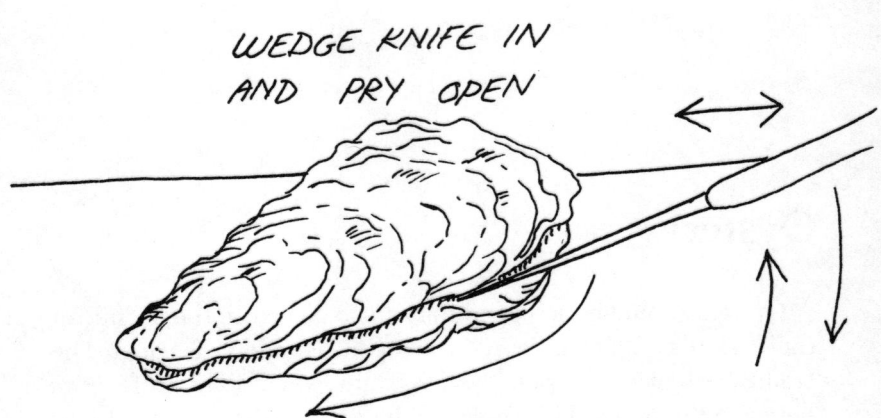

WEDGE KNIFE IN AND PRY OPEN

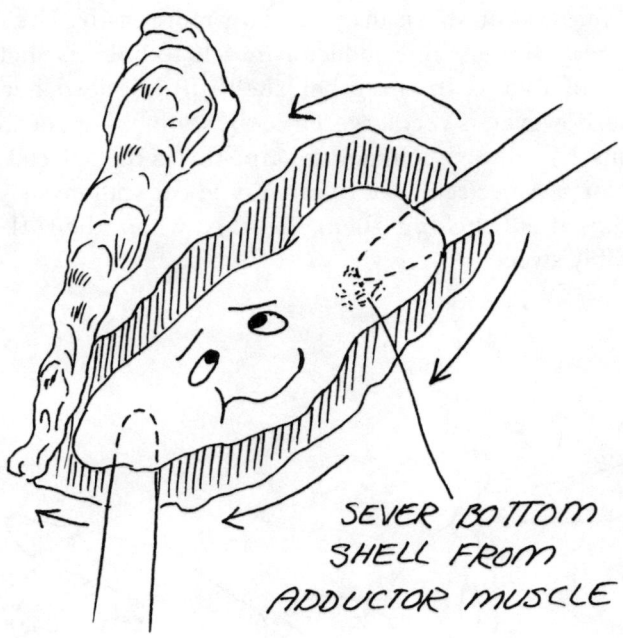

SEVER BOTTOM SHELL FROM ADDUCTOR MUSCLE

Cut the muscles and pry the shell open. Often, however, it is very difficult to wedge your knife between the shells. So try brute force. Place the oyster on a table with its round shell up. Take a hammer or wooden mallet and rap the edge of the shells until a piece breaks off, leaving an opening. Then insert your knife and go to work. Once the oyster is open, wash it off under the tap. Scoop out the flesh by cutting in from the shell.

You can store oysters for many days, even weeks, under the right conditions. They should be kept cool and moist. One way is to wrap them in burlap inside a pail and keep them dampened with sea water. Another is to refrigerate them, remembering to dampen them, with salt water if possible.

Scallops

First, scrub the scallops under cold water. You can then open them much as you shuck an oyster, only more easily. The scallop, by the way, has just one adductor muscle to hold its shells fast, instead of two as in the other shellfish described here. The muscle, however, is very large. Once the scallop is opened, cut out the muscle and wash it under the tap—this is the delectable part that North Americans like to eat. Try to eat scallops as soon as you can after catching them. This is when their flavor is incredibly sweet.

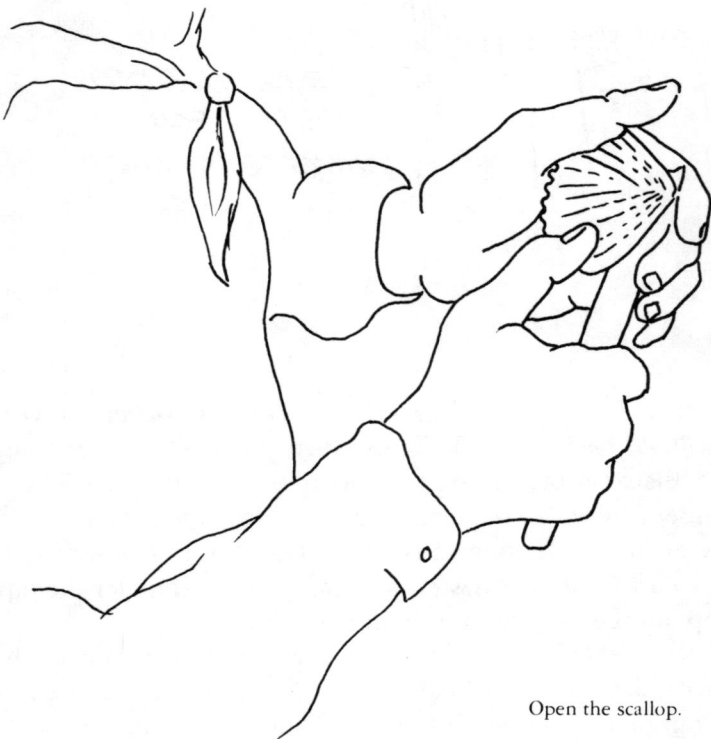

Open the scallop.

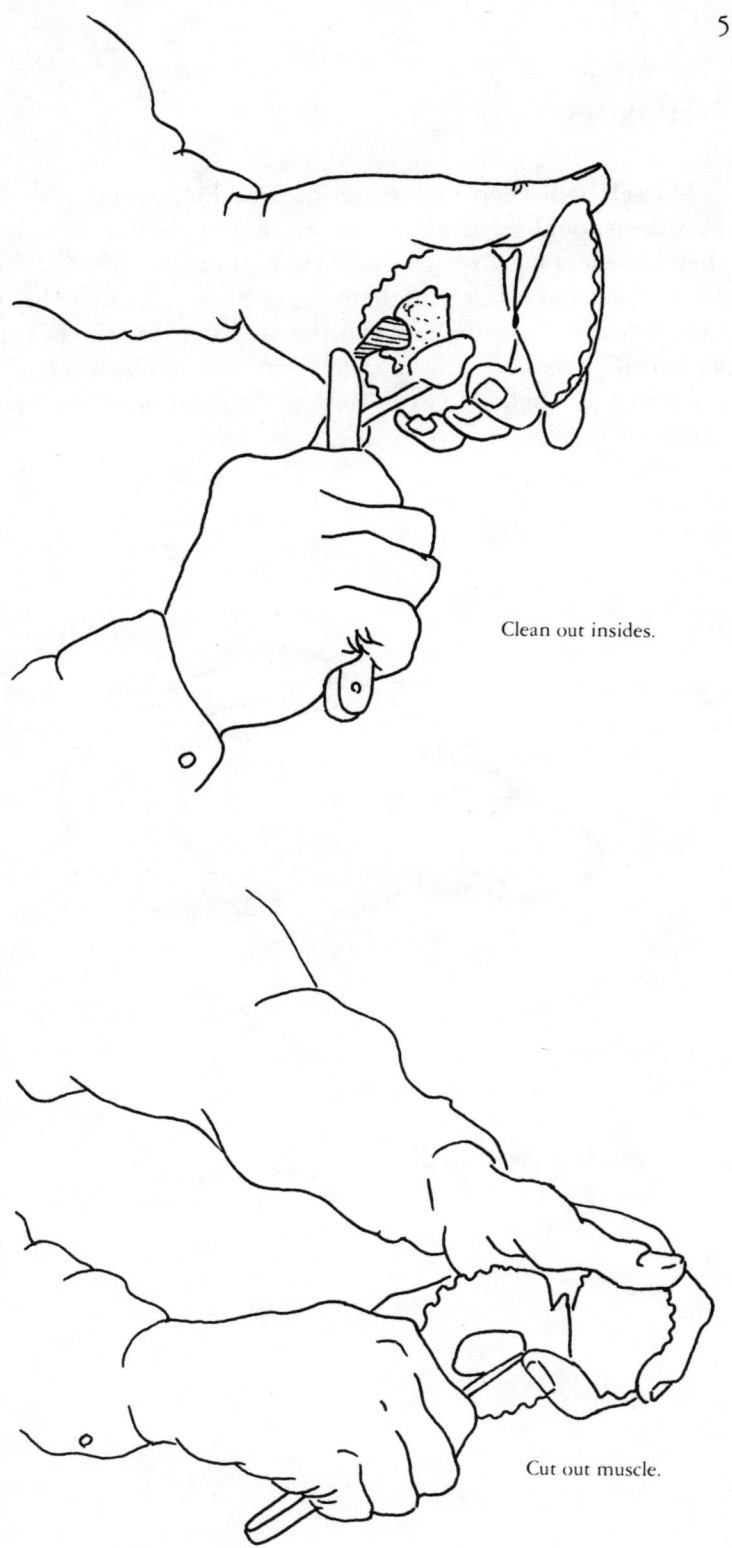

Mussels

Mussels will keep in the refrigerator for several days. The outsides should be scrubbed under running water. Internally, they have less debris than other clams, but they often must be scraped with a knife. Open them the same way as other shellfish except work the knife between the shells where the byssus is located. The seal is not as hard to break here as elsewhere along the rim of the shell. After you take out the meat, wash it off and it is ready to cook.

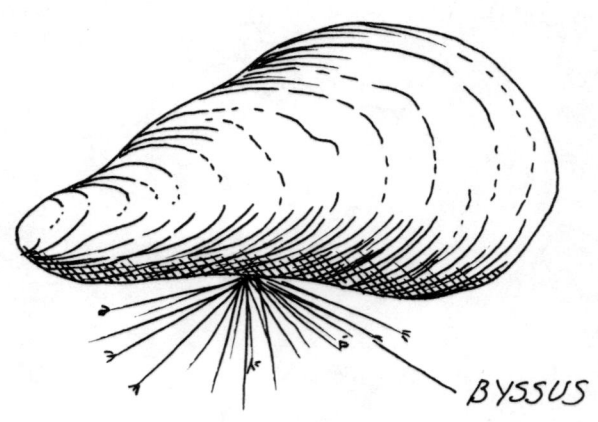

BLUE MUSSEL (2"-3")

6. COOKING YOUR CATCH

Raw or Cooked

Some of the shellfish described here are delectable either raw or cooked. The following should be cooked:
- Razor clam (any clam recipe)
- Surf clam (any clam recipe)
- Soft-shell clam
- Blue mussel

Hard-shell clams, oysters, and scallops can be offered at the table either raw or cooked.

Shellfish on the Halfshell

Rinse the shells of oysters and hard-shell clams after the soft parts have been removed. Then replace the meat and serve. Spice up with red wine vinegar, lemon juice, hot sauce, or cocktail sauce. Eat directly from the shell.

Raw Scallops

The adductor muscles of scallops can be eaten as is. Lime juice peps them up.

New England Clam Chowder

3 quarts shucked clams
¼ pound diced salt pork
   or bacon
2 cups chopped onion
2 cups chopped celery
2 quarts diced potatoes

2 bay leaves
1½ tablespoons salt
½ teaspoon pepper
2½ quarts hot milk
¼ cup margarine or butter

Drain clams and save liquor. Remove any shell particles and chop clams. Fry salt pork or bacon until crisp. Add onion and celery and cook until tender. Add potatoes, bay leaves, salt, and pepper. Cover and bring to the boiling point; simmer about 20 minutes or until potatoes are tender. Add chopped clams and liquor and cook an additional 5 to 10 minutes or until clams are done. Add milk and margarine; heat until hot enough to serve. Remove bay leaves. Serve using a 1-cup ladle. Garnish with chopped parsley. Serves 25.

Manhattan Clam Chowder

3 quarts shucked clams
¼ pound diced salt pork
   or bacon
2 cups chopped onion
2 quarts diced potatoes
2 cans (1 pound, 12 ounces
   each) tomatoes*

1 quart hot water
1 tablespoon salt
½ teaspoon pepper
¼ cup margarine or butter
¼ cup chopped parsley

Drain clams and save liquor. Remove any shell particles and chop clams. Fry salt pork or bacon until crisp in large heavy pot or saucepan. Add onion and celery and cook until tender. Add potatoes, tomatoes or tomato juice, and water. Cover and bring to the boiling point; simmer about 20 minutes or until potatoes are tender. Add chopped clams and liquor, salt and pepper, and cook an additional 5 to 10 minutes or until clams are done. Add margarine; heat. Serve using a 1-cup ladle. Garnish with chopped parsley. Serves 25.

*Note: 2 quarts tomato juice may be substituted in place of the tomatoes.

Souper Clam Dandy

2 cans (7½ or 8 ounces each) minced clams
1 package (10 ounces) frozen baby lima beans
1 cup boiling water
½ teaspoon savory salt
4 slices bacon
2 cans (10½ ounces each) condensed cream of chicken soup
1½ cups milk
1 tablespoon onion powder
Dash liquid hot pepper sauce

Drain clams. Place beans in boiling salted water in a 3-quart saucepan. Bring to the boiling point again. Cover and simmer for 10 to 15 minutes or until beans are tender. Fry bacon until crisp. Drain on absorbent paper. Crumble bacon. When beans are tender, stir in remaining ingredients except bacon. Cover and simmer until hot. Garnish soup with bacon. Serves 6.

New England Clambake

6 dozen steamer clams
12 small onions
6 medium baking potatoes
6 ears of corn in the husks
6 live lobsters (1 pound each)
Rockweed (optional)
Lemon wedges
Melted butter or margarine

Wash clam shells thoroughly. Peel onions and wash potatoes. Parboil onions and potatoes for 15 minutes; drain. Remove corn silk from corn and replace husks. Cut 12 pieces of cheesecloth and 12 pieces of heavy-duty aluminum foil, 18 x 36 inches each. Place 2 pieces of cheesecloth on top of 2 pieces of foil. Place 2 onions, a potato, ear of corn, lobster, 1 dozen clams, and rockweed on cheesecloth. Tie opposite corners of cheesecloth together. Pour 1 cup of water over the package. Bring foil up over the food and close all edges with tight double folds. Make 6 packages. Place packages on a grill about 4 inches from hot coals. Cover with hood or aluminum foil. Cook for 45 to 60 minutes or until onions and potatoes are cooked. Open packages and crack lobster claws. Serve with lemon wedges and melted butter. Serves 6.

Chesapeake Bay Clambake

6 dozen soft-shell clams
12 small onions
6 medium baking potatoes
6 ears of corn in the husks
12 live, hard-shell blue crabs
Lemon wedges
Melted butter or margarine

Wash clam shells thoroughly. Peel onions and wash potatoes. Parboil onions and potatoes for 15 minutes; drain. Remove corn silk from corn and replace husks. Cut 12 pieces of cheesecloth and 12 pieces of heavy-duty aluminum foil, 18 x 36 inches each. Place 2 pieces of cheesecloth on top of 2 pieces of foil. Place 2 onions, a potato, ear of corn, 1 dozen clams, and 2 crabs on cheesecloth. Tie opposite corners of the cheesecloth together. Pour 1 cup of water over the package. Bring foil up over the food and close all edges with tight double folds. Make 6 packages. Place packages on a grill about 4 inches from hot coals. Cover with hood or aluminum foil. Cook for 45 to 60 minutes or until onions and potatoes are cooked. Serve with lemon wedges and butter. Serves 6.

Pilgrims' Clam Pie

3 dozen shell clams
  or
3 cans (8 ounces each) minced clams
1½ cups water
¼ cup margarine or butter
½ cup sliced fresh mushrooms
2 tablespoons minced onion
¼ cup all-purpose flour
⅛ teaspoon liquid hot pepper sauce
¼ teaspoon dry mustard
¼ teaspoon salt
⅛ teaspoon white pepper
1 cup reserved clam liquor
1 cup half and half
1 tablespoon lemon juice
2 tablespoons chopped parsley
2 tablespoons chopped pimiento
Pastry for a 1-crust 9-inch pie
1 egg, beaten

Wash clam shells thoroughly. Place clams in a large pot with water. Bring to a boil and simmer for 8 to 10 minutes or until clams open. Remove clams from shell and cut into fourths. Reserve 1 cup clam liquor. (OR: If using canned clams, drain and reserve 1 cup liquor). In a skillet melt margarine. Add mushrooms and onion and cook until tender. Stir in flour, mustard, liquid hot pepper sauce, salt, and pepper. Gradually add clam liquor and half and half. Cook, stirring constantly, until thick. Stir in lemon juice, parsley, pimiento, and clams. Pour mixture into a 9-inch round deep-dish pie plate (about 2 inches deep). Roll out pastry dough and place on top of mixture in pie plate; secure dough to the rim of the pie plate by crimping. Vent pastry. Brush with beaten egg. Bake in a hot oven, 375° F., for 25 to 30 minutes or until pastry is browned. Serves 6.

Surf Clam Muscles

1½ pounds surf clam muscles
½ cup white wine
¼ tablespoon salt
1 tablespoon minced onions
4 drops hot sauce

Fresh salted butter
3 tablespoons flour
½ cup heavy cream
1 cup grated sharp cheddar cheese
½ cup dark bread crumbs

Wash surf clam muscles in clam juice and place in pan with wine, salt, onions, hot sauce, and pepper. Bring to a boil, cover, and simmer for 10 minutes. Drain and save 1 cup of the broth. In the same pan, melt butter, blend in flour, and then add the broth and cream. Stir constantly. After the mixture has thickened, add grated cheese and clam muscles. Put in a casserole and sprinkle the top with bread crumbs. Bake at 400° F. for 10 minutes.

Oyster Stuffing

1 pint oysters, chopped with liquor
1 medium to large onion, chopped
½ cup butter or margarine
8 slices day-old bread, cubed
1 teaspoon salt
⅛ teaspoon pepper

Cook onion and celery in margarine or butter until almost tender. Add chopped oysters and liquor. Cook until oyster edges curl. Add remaining ingredients, mixing thoroughly. Moisten as desired with oyster liquor. For a 10-15-pound turkey, use 3 times above recipe.

Oyster Stew

1 pint oysters, drained
4 tablespoons butter
1 quart milk
1½ teaspoon salt
⅛ teaspoon pepper
Paprika

Melt butter, add oysters, and cook 3 minutes or until edges curl. Add milk, salt, and pepper, and bring almost to boiling. Serve at once. Serves 6.

Oyster Kabobs

1 dozen oysters, drained
1 dozen fresh mushroom caps
1 large green pepper
3 strips bacon
¼ pound butter, melted

Cut bacon and pepper into bite-sized squares. Skewer oyster, bacon, mushroom cap, and green pepper on toothpicks. Place in a shallow baking dish with melted butter. Bake at 450° F for 15 minutes or until bacon browns.

Fried Oysters

1 quart oysters, drained
2 eggs, slightly beaten
2 tablespoons milk

1 teaspoon salt
1/8 teaspoon pepper
1 cup bread crumbs or cornmeal

Mix eggs, milk, and seasonings. Dip oysters in egg mixture and roll in crumbs. Fry in hot fat 5 minutes, turning one time until both sides brown. Drain on absorbent paper. Serves 6.

Oyster Scallop

4 tablespoons butter or margarine
2 cups soda cracker crumbs (about 24)
1/2 cup chopped parsley
1/4 teaspoon pepper

1 pint (about 24) oysters or two cans (7 ounces each) frozen oysters, thawed
1/2 cup light or table cream
1 teaspoon Worcestershire sauce

Melt butter in saucepan; remove from heat. Stir in cracker crumbs, parsley, salt, and pepper. Drain and save juice from oysters. Sprinkle 1/3 of crumb mixture into a 9-inch pie plate, layer half of oysters on top, and then add half of remaining crumbs and rest of oysters. Combine saved oyster juice, cream, and Worcestershire sauce, and pour over top. Sprinkle with remaining crumbs. Bake at 350° F. for 30 minutes or until top is golden. Serve hot, plain or with chili sauce. Serves 4 to 6.

Oyster Surprise

1 pint oysters, drained
3 slices bacon
3 tablespoons chopped onion
1½ tablespoons chopped green pepper
1 teaspoon lemon juice
½ teaspoon salt
½ teaspoon pepper
½ teaspoon Worcestershire sauce
Dash Tabasco sauce
1 stalk celery, diced

Chop bacon and fry until brown. Drain on paper. In hot bacon fat, fry onion, green pepper, and celery until tender. Add seasonings. Mix well. In a greased baking dish, arrange the oysters and spread mixture over the oysters. Crumble bacon over top. Bake at 350° F. for 8 to 10 minutes.

Oyster Bisque

1 pint oysters
½ small onion, diced
2 stalks celery, diced
1/3 cup flour
2 teaspoons salt
1 quart milk
1 bay leaf, crushed
1/3 cup butter
¼ teaspoon pepper

Drain and save liquor from oysters. Chop oysters fine. Add liquor and heat until edges curl. Scald milk with bay leaf, onion, and celery. Drain through a colander. Melt butter; blend in flour. Mix with milk and cook until thickened, stirring frequently. Add oysters. Let set 1 minute and serve.

Opulent Oysters

3 cans (8 ounces each) oysters
1 can (3½ ounces) French-fried onions
¼ cup light cream
2 tablespoons grated Parmesan cheese
2 tablespoons butter or margarine

Drain oysters thoroughly. Spread ¾ cup of onions in a well-greased round baking dish, 8 x 2 inches. Cover with the oysters. Pour cream over oysters. Combine remaining onions and cheese, and sprinkle over top. Dot with butter. Bake in a very hot oven, 450° F., for 8 to 10 minutes or until lightly browned. Serves 6.

Charcoal-Broiled Scallops

2 pounds scallops, fresh or frozen
½ cup melted fat or oil
¼ cup lemon juice
2 teaspoons salt
¼ teaspoon white pepper
½ pound sliced bacon
Paprika

Thaw frozen scallops. Rinse with cold water to remove any shell particles. Place scallops in a bowl. Combine fat, lemon juice, salt, and pepper. Pour sauce over scallops and let stand for 30 minutes, stirring occasionally. Cut each slice of bacon in half lengthwise and then crosswise. Remove scallops, reserving sauce for basting. Wrap each scallop with a piece of bacon and fasten with a toothpick. Place scallops in well-greased, hinged wire grills. Sprinkle with paprika. Cook about 4 inches from moderately hot coals for 5 minutes. Baste with sauce and sprinkle with paprika. Turn and cook for 5 to 7 minutes longer or until bacon is crisp. Serves 6.

Scallop Kabobs

1 pound scallops, fresh or frozen
1 can (13½ ounces) pineapple chunks, drained
1 can (4 ounces) button mushrooms, drained
1 green pepper, cut into 1-inch squares
¼ cup melted fat or oil
¼ cup lemon juice
¼ cup chopped parsley
¼ cup soy sauce
½ teaspoon salt
Dash pepper
12 slices bacon

Thaw frozen scallops. Rinse with cold water to remove any shell particles. Place pineapple, mushrooms, green pepper, and scallops in a bowl. Combine fat, lemon juice, parsley, soy sauce, salt, and pepper. Pour sauce over scallop mixture and let stand for 30 minutes, stirring occasionally. Fry bacon until cooked but not crisp. Cut each slice in half. Using long skewers, alternate scallops, pineapple, mushrooms, green pepper, and bacon until skewers are filled. cook about 4 inches from moderately hot coals for 5 minutes. Baste with sauce. Turn and cook for 5 to 7 minutes longer or until bacon is crisp. Serves 6.

Skewered Scallops

1 pound scallops, fresh or frozen
1 pint cherry tomatoes
2 large green peppers
1/3 cup lemon juice
3 tablespoons honey
3 tablespoons prepared mustard
2 tablespoons melted fat or oil
1½ teaspoons curry powder

Thaw frozen scallops. Rinse with cold water to remove any shell particles. Cut large scallops in half. Wash tomatoes and green peppers. Cut green peppers into 1-inch squares. Alternate scallops, tomatoes, and green pepper on 40 skewers or round toothpicks approximately 3 inches long. Place kabobs on a well-greased broiler pan. Combine remaining ingredients. Brush kabobs with sauce. Broil about 4 inches from source of heat for 5 to 7 minutes. Turn carefully and brush with sauce. Broil 5 to 7 minutes longer, basting once. Makes approximately 40 hors d'oeuvres.

Point Judith Scallops

1 pound scallops, fresh or frozen
¼ cup margarine or butter
1 cup sliced fresh mushrooms
¼ cup margarine or butter
2 tablespoons minced onion
2 tablespoons all-purpose flour
½ teaspoon salt
4 egg yolks, beaten
½ teaspoon leaf thyme
¼ teaspoon basil leaves
½ cup fresh bread crumbs
1/3 cup grated Swiss Gruyere cheese
¼ teaspoon paprika
1 tablespoon melted margarine or butter
1½ cups half and half

Thaw scallops if frozen. Remove any shell particles and wash. In a skillet melt margarine. Add scallops and mushrooms. Cook for 3 to 4 minutes or until scallops are done. Divide scallops and mushrooms into 6 individual shells or ramekins. In a small saucepan melt ¼ cup margarine. Add onion and cook until tender. Stir in flour and salt. Gradually stir in half and half. Cook until thickened, stirring constantly. Add a little of the hot sauce to the egg yolks; add to remaining sauce, stirring constantly. Heat just until thickened. Stir in thyme and basil. Spoon sauce over scallops. Combine bread crumbs, cheese, paprika, and margarine. Sprinkle on top of sauce. Place shells on a baking tray and bake in a hot oven, 400° F., for 10 to 15 minutes or until hot and bubbly. Serves 6.

Fried Mussels

Mussels
Flour
Garlic sauce

Olive oil
Salt and pepper

Scrub the mussels thoroughly. Wash in clear water. Place in a deep kettle without water and cover. Cook over high heat until the shells open (4 to 6 minutes). Remove the meat from the shells and roll in flour that has been seasoned with salt and pepper. Fry in olive oil until golden brown. Drain on absorbent paper and serve at once, with garlic sauce.

Mussels with Tomatoes

Mussels
Tomatoes

Bread crumbs
Salt and pepper

Steam open the mussels, remove from the shells, and, for each pound of mussel meat, take 2 tomatoes, dice them, and fry them in a little butter with a tablespoon of bread crumbs; season with salt and pepper. When done, add the mussels with a little liquor in which they were cooked. Mix and serve hot.

Mussel Casserole

This surprisingly excellent recipe can be made precisely like an ordinary chicken and noodle casserole except that 1 pound of cleaned mussels is substituted for the chicken. If, after being heated for 40 minutes in a 350° F. oven, it becomes too dry, undiluted canned mushroom soup may be poured over it to remedy the situation.

Mussels in Batter

Mussels
Olive oil
Lemon juice
Minced parsley
Batter

Sprinkle freshly cleaned and steamed mussels with a mixture of olive oil and lemon juice. Roll in chopped parsley and drain. Then dip in any good frying batter and fry in deep fat until brown. Serve hot, garnished with parsley and a helping of potato salad.

Mussel Soup

White part of 2 leeks, chopped
1 onion, chopped
4 tablespoons olive oil
Liquor from 6 pounds of steamed mussels
Mince parsley
¾ cup rice
Bay leaf
Pinch of saffron
Pinch of cayenne
Mussel meat

Fry leeks and onion in oil till golden. Add mussel liquor. When it boils, add rice and seasonings. Cook 20 minutes over low heat, remove bay leaf, and add mussels. Garnish with minced parsley and serve hot.

Stuffed Mussels

3 dozen mussels
2 large onions, minced
1 cup olive oil
¾ cup long grain rice, washed and drained
1 tomato, peeled and minced
2 tablespoons pine nuts
Generous ½ teaspoon of allspice
Salt and pepper to taste

    Scrub the outside of the mussel shells. Rinse. Open with the point of a sharp knife and remove any hair present. Rinse thoroughly. Loosen the joints so that the shells will remain closed after stuffing. Saute the minced onions in olive oil in a saucepan until transparent. Add the rest of the ingredients and mix thoroughly. When cool enough to handle, place a spoonful of stuffing into each shell (not too full, to allow for expansion of rice). Close the shells and place in layers in a deep pan. Cover with a glass pie plate and pour 2 cups of water over the plate. Cover the pan and simmer over low heat for 1½ to 1¾ hours or until the rice is cooked. Remove from pan and cool. Place in refrigerator to chill. Serve with lemon. Serves 6.

Sea Sauce

1 can (8 ounces) tomato sauce
¼ cup chili sauce
¼ teaspoon garlic powder
¼ teaspoon oregano
¼ teaspoon liquid hot pepper sauce
¼ teaspoon thyme
⅛ teaspoon sugar
Dash basil

    Combine all ingredients. Simmer 10 to 12 minutes, stirring occasionally. Makes approximately 1 cup sauce.

Notes

Record the date, time of day, and how long pots set, bait, weather, location, depth, distance from shore and *catch*.
GOOD RECORDS MAKE FOR GOOD CATCHES.

Notes

Notes

Notes

Notes

Notes

Notes

Notes

Notes

Notes